Let the Rail Splitter Awake

Pablo Neruda

Let the Rail Splitter Awake and other poems

introduction by
Christopher Perriam
illustrations by
José Venturelli

Journeyman

First published in Great Britain
by the Journeyman Press Limited

The Journeyman Press Ltd, 97 Ferme Park Road
Crouch End, London, N8 9SA

Originally published in Spanish in the *Canto general*
Mexico City, 1950. This selection translated and published by
Masses & Mainstream, New York, 1950

Journeyman *Chapbook* 10

British Library Cataloguing in Publication Data

Neruda, Pablo
    Let the rail splitter awake and other poems.
    Rn: Neftali Ricardo Reyes Basualto
    I. Title   II. Perriam, Christopher
    861   PQ8097.N4

    ISBN 1-85172-009-7

First printing 1988
10 9 8 7 6 5 4 3 2 1

Cover designed by Ingrid Vandergucht

Computer typeset from disc in Palatino 10/12
by Wordstream Ltd, Poole and printed in Great Britain
by Richard Clay Ltd, Bungay, Suffolk

CONTENTS

Introduction   7

LET THE RAIL SPLITTER AWAKE   19

TO MIGUEL HERNÁNDEZ,
MURDERED IN THE PRISONS OF SPAIN   39

THE DEAD IN THE SQUARE   45

SONG FOR BOLIVAR   55

THE FUGITIVE   59

THE HEIGHTS OF MACCHU PICCHU   77

A further note   91

INTRODUCTION

Speaking to the Stockholm audience on his acceptance of the Nobel Prize for literature in December 1971, Pablo Neruda likened his native Chile, stretching down towards the South Pole, to Sweden, 'its head just touching the snowy north of the planet'. The *Canto general*, from which the poems in this anthology are translated, had begun as a 'Song of Chile' but when it was completed, it too had expanded, reaching out northwards across the whole of Latin America. Being a socialist creation story, it intended to embrace the world, mythologically reinterpreting history, destroying imperialist and capitalist myths and moulding the powerful symbolism of Christianity into a new Marxist language. It also gave back identity — to the peoples of Latin America, to poetry, and, as 'The Heights of Macchu Picchu' makes clear, to the poet himself.

When *Let the Rail Splitter Awake and other poems* was originally published in 1950 (hard on the publication of the *Canto general*), it translated Neruda's poems into a very particular context. It addressed the North American people at the height of the Cold War. Intending to raise consciousness then, it still holds the power to do so now and has gained a new topicality. Writing in the 1973 'Incitation to Nixonicide and Song of Praise to the Chilean Revolution' Neruda called for help from Walt Whitman and implicitly that other North America — just as he had done in the poem 'Let the Rail Splitter Awake'. Not only must Neruda himself, in the last year of his life, have been shocked and distressed to recall his earlier condemnation of North American foreign policy and to see how little things had changed, but to his readers now, in the late-1980s, it is an all-too-familiar picture which is painted in 'Let the Rail Splitter Awake': 'They want to keep on selling

/ steel and bullets. . .', ' "they" mix cocktails with drops / from the song "Let us defend Christian culture" ' (section II) and they have to be angrily warned 'Do not enter Nicaragua either, / Sandino sleeps in the forest until your coming' — Sandino has in a sense awoken now, and the *Sandinistas* are carrying on their struggle. Shockingly familiar too is the scenario of 'The Dead in the Square', composed soon after the tragic events of 28 January 1946. It is not only history's recurrences which make these poems of lasting interest; Neruda's politics are above all lyrical, yet certainly none the less active and committed for that.

Pablo Neruda was born in Parral, just north of Chillán, in 1904, in a 'land laden with grapes' (as he called it in 'Birth', the first poem in the autobiographical *Notebook from Isla Negra* of 1964). He was brought up in Temuco (further south) and in the second poem of the *Notebook*, 'The First Voyage', he characterises the place and his relationship to it: 'under the axe and the rain the timber city grew. . .', 'my heart still fells the forest there / and sings with the saws on the wood in the rain / milling the cold, and the sawdust and the scent'. It was here, in his teens, that he made a first symbolic bid for poetic identity by adopting the name Pablo Neruda (he was christened Neftalí Ricardo Basoalto Reyes). This early gesture was formalised by deed poll in December 1946, the year after he had been elected to the Chilean Senate, had joined the Communist Party and had written 'The Heights of Macchu Picchu'.

In 1948, after an open denunciation of President González Videla (whose 'Law for the Permanent Defence of Democracy' outlawed the Communist Party), Neruda was forced into clandestinity. 'The Fugitive' (1949) tells of this period of the poet's life and is autobiography, miniature history of contemporary Chile and an allegory all at once: like 'The Heights of Macchu Picchu', it is a development of the concept of solidarity, a discovery made by way of a spiritual (and real) journey. 'The Heights of Macchu Picchu' was written at the poet's home at Isla Negra, facing the Pacific, and this place became the scene of ever more intense investigations of the individual's relationship to the world and to words in the poems of the 1960s and early

1970s. It was at Isla Negra that his dying days were spent in 1973, coinciding with the dying days of Salvador Allende's Marxist coalition government.

At Stockholm, and earlier in 'Let the Rail Splitter Awake', Neruda spoke as 'a poet from the extreme south of America / son of a rail-road worker from Patagonia, / American as the Andean air' (III). Chile is the touchstone and the point of departure. Contemplating Whitman's and Lincoln's North America he states, 'there, from within my central rock of being / I could extend my eyes, ears, hands on the air' (I). The foundations of Neruda's identity, in the 1940s and 1950s at least, is inseparably political and lyrical: in the poem 'To My Party' he tells the Communist Party that 'You have made me indestructible, for I no longer end in myself'; equally rocks and stones, as 'The Heights of Macchu Picchu' shows, are essential markers in a wide emotional landscape. Grapes and timber, stones, waves and rain are powerful elements in the lyricized Chile which emerges from Neruda's poetry. At the same time, too, they are signs of solidarity: the personal becomes political. The regional becomes global. Extension is the key concept: Chile does not end in itself, the self — 'myself' — does not either. The extreme south inevitably reaches out to the north, wanting both to differentiate itself from it politically and to join it, having redeemed it. Entering into an ideal dialogue between the West and the East, defying the silences of the Cold War, 'I', the poetic voice, is subsumed into a trans-continental conversation, helped, in this anthology's case, by the translators who brought the poems across frontiers of language, helping in Neruda's grand project of expansion and extension.

In 'Let the Rail Splitter Awake', North America is linked to the Soviet Union in a kind of lyrical dialogue constructed of parallel images. The symbolic 'children of Stalingrad', 'steely, smiling, / ready for song or combat' (IV) are set in a relationship of correspondence with 'the young white, the young Negro' who will 'sing ... and conquer' under the sign of the axe of the benign patriarch Abe Lincoln (V); a tractor on the plains of the Far West (I) corresponds to one on the plains of Russia (III); factories in the East corres-

Que Despierte el Leñador (later *Canto general*: IX) clandestine first edition
published in Chile, August 1948 (*reproduced with kind permission of Robert
Pring-Mill*)

pond to factories in the West; Brooklyn and Kiev are twinned, Juana and Jane, Juan and John are linked (III).

The vital, unifying third point in the triangle is Chile, and in it Pablo Neruda. The Ural pines (III) with their aroma lead us back south; the revolution has all 'the fire of the Araucanian volcanoes' (III); Lincoln, in North America, 'with his axe' (V), is no mere political hero but a metaphorical bridge: Lincoln the woodsman is close to that heart of Neruda's which 'sings with the saws on the wood in the rain'. The 'dense / steel aroma' of the woods of Tacoma (I) link East to the Ural pines and to the steely voice of triumph of the Soviet Revolution and back to the woods of southern Chile, and to that powerful voice from the 'extreme south'.

Importantly, the aroma propagated from the three sources reminds Neruda of his place in a literary revolution too. 'From the fragrant Ural pines' he watches 'the library which is being born / in the heart of Russia' and sees — smells — books, 'books / in fresh shelves of pine and cedar' (III). Taking part with him in the multifarious propaganda of the *Canto general*, and alongside the songs and chants of millions, are indeed voices out of books. Whitman is there in name, along with others in 'Let the Rail Splitter Awake' (I); and in this poem and 'Song for Bolivar' (1941) there are strong echoes in theme and style of two hugely influential voices — those of the poets José Martí (Cuba: 1853-95) and Rubén Darío (Nicaragua: 1867-1916), both, in different ways, impassioned protestors against imperialism.

The recurring images of the earth, the elements, blood, rebirth and song also link these poems to a vast body of texts written and orally transmitted — to the songs, ballads, verses and poems of Republican Spain in the Civil War (which had found Neruda in Spain as Chilean consul, an important radicalising experience). Beyond these texts, Neruda reaches out to make contact with the whole wide language of the Revolution coming to Spain both directly from the Soviet Union and through France. Miguel Hernández (Orihuela, Murcia Province, 1910-42) is one voice which encapsulated this. Again, in 'To Miguel Hernández Murdered in the Prisons of Spain' (1950), an aroma is the key which allows communication: 'You come to me straight from the East, Goatherd' (in this case the East-West connection is from Hernández's native Levante region — where he had tended his family's goats — northwest to Madrid, as well as from Spain to Chile), 'you / brought me ... / ... an aroma of Fray Luis, of orange blossoms, of dung / burning in the mountains'. These lines acutely capture the sweet-acrid character of Hernández's writing — and, in their mix of earthiness and sensitivity are typical of Neruda. Along with a quotation of one of the Spanish poet's most memorable juxtapositions — 'nightingale and rifle' — they effectively bring this other voice from the North and East into the *Canto general*. With it too, comes Fray Luis de León (Belmonte, Castile: 1527-91), reminding us of a further chorus of voices — the Spanish poets of the Golden Age, and in particular Francisco de Quevedo (Madrid: 1580-1645) whom Neruda discovered at the start of the Spanish Civil War and from whom he learned a certain witty, incisive, bitter and perversely beautiful manner. Quevedo, in fact, might be said to be the power behind many of Neruda's surprising, revealing linkages of ideas.

One such linkage comes in 'The Dead in the Square'. The poem is about the gunning-down of a crowd demonstrating in solidarity with the protesting workers of the northern nitrate mines, at Mapocho and Humberston. The incident occurred on 28 January 1946, in the Square outside the Moneda Palace in Santiago (where Salvador Allende was to meet his death in September 1973). Neruda had written an earlier text on the events, which was accompanied by the Chilean José Venturelli's impressive illustrations reproduced in this anthology (*28 de enero*, published by the Comisíon Nacional de Prensa, Cultura y Propaganda del Partido Comunista, 1947). As the Communist Party's candidate in the northern province, Neruda was closely involved with the struggle of the workers there. The poem is a vivid poem of witness, remarkably visual in its rhetoric — a feature emphasized by Venturelli. Neruda's faces of Chile 'wearing / the signature of pain' (I) are there in his powerful images. The people united by duty,

12

love and the common canto (VI and IX) stand out symbolically in Venturelli's unifying blocks and lines.

The poet and artist are collaborators: Venturelli's Chilean worker holding the banner with a hammer and sickle motif, one corner dipped in the pool of blood on the ground, can be seen as an emblem to Neruda's text. There, the blood first appears in section II, 'the drops of my people's blood', which before, as III describes it, 'had been hidden ... always washed off and forgotten' but which now 'burned like fire'. In order to make this blood a perpetual, shining revelation of the truth, in VI it becomes 'like stars, fixed and implacable' — an effective challenge to any sordid cover-up attempts by the oppressors. In VII these stars are interwoven with the visual image of the Chilean flag: 'they cut out from their shirts, or perhaps from a fold of the sky / that patch of blue to hold the star of their country' — and by their joint metaphorical action (backed by real defiance in word and deed) of poet and people, drawing the threads together, the bottom half of the flag turns victorious red. It takes on the colours of the stars, and their fire. So Venturelli's banner and the banner in sections VIII and IX is not simply a one message banner. Being the colour of the stain of old blood spilled by crimes of oppression and the colour of new blood, it tells of a whole history redeemed by the people: by its presence and their action the colour red changes from a negative to a positive sign as the threads are drawn together. Chile is extended to the whole socialist world: Ramona Parra — 'a new star in our sky' — is taken up by the symbolism and becomes a sign of a new heaven and a new earth; and César Tapia's (anyone's) death and blood become, in the bellying red membranes of the banners in the wind, the rhythm, the systole and diastole of freedom. Death blood becomes life blood. Personal tragedy becomes the people's triumph.

Images constantly reach out and connect like this in the *Canto general*, in a process which is both the product and the producer of Neruda's fundamental, expansive, unifying and intuitively socialist approach. So we find in the relatively early 'Song for Bolívar' (1941) Bolívar disseminated throughout South America, Bolivar reached out to by hands across the sea from Republican Spain, Bolivar's memory as a red rose to match Ramona Parra whose blood flowers to freedom, Bolivar with his banner 'embroidered with blood', Bolivar as another face in the crowd of faces 'wearing / the signature of pain', and as a voice speaking out of the mouth of the militant and the dead.

At the very centre of what is an enormously complicated system of linkages is the sequence 'The Heights of Macchu Picchu'. This is a poem which is many things at once and which deliberately provokes a multitude of possible approaches to its core idea, that of overcoming personal and collective alienation. It begins by leading its reader through a many-sided experience in which normal concepts of sense, of space and time are subverted. There are clues — streets, a wood, a field, a 'buried tower', the sea; autumn, spring, night, day, moonrise. We cannot tell, however, where we are nor where to go. This first canto is variously the description of a present crisis of identity (we are sharing the writer's own disorientation); a narrative of crisis undergone, and a glimpse of the light at the end of the tunnel; the first in a sequence of five cantos (I to V) recalling the specific crisis of Neruda's surrealistic-existential poetry of 1925-1935; and the preamble to the rest of the poem, a kind of rehearsal for the poem's enactment of an exorcism of past confusions and its emergence into clarity. That 'someone who waited for me among the violins' is a representation of the poet's own fragmented identity — he meets himself meeting himself in this poem, and picks up the pieces. At the same time it is an anticipation of the great and moving encounter with the rest of humanity living and dead which comes later in the poem. The early spiralling down (I) is countered by the ascent to Macchu Picchu — the majestic Inca citadel — and by a different sort of delving down, one which can only be done from the vantage point of that summit of experience, a delving down into the history and the prehistory of the *pueblo* and the land. The intensely erotico-mystical penetration committed among the romantic and nostalgic violins and jasmine (I) leads out to the powerful, liberating, public love affair with all America in Canto VIII.

Cantos II to V make two major discoveries on the path to the symbolic reunion. Canto II identifies the poet's past false consciousness, and III sees a whole world of hollow men, alienated by their labour; in IV it becomes clear that redemption and fulfilment can now be seen as having depended on communication, on the recognition by each individual that they are part, organic part, of the 'tree of the *pueblo*' (a key symbol in the *Canto general*). This discovery of a personal and collective loss goes hand in hand with the discovery, in III and V, that there are two ways of death — small, paltry, private and meaningless, or grandiose and 'grave'. This greater death is properly defined and discovered only after the ascent to the birthplace of humanity in Canto VI and the stunning encounter with the assembled dead in VII.

Like the Soviet peoples in 'Let the Rail Splitter Awake', the dead of Macchu Picchu form 'all one vast high wall of stone and blood' (section IV of 'Let the Rail Splitter Awake'): they are there as part of a 'permanence of stone and word' (Canto VII). The river Wilkamayu, seen from the Heights, carries 'words', 'syllables' and 'banners' (VIII) in its 'arterial waters' and so a link is made between these dead and the 'Dead in the Square'. The dead who live again at Macchu Picchu (and who revitalise the poet as individual) have been crushed by oppression, exploitation and hunger (X), their blood has been covered up like that of those Chileans. As Neruda approaches them more and more closely (in XI), the blood flows again: 'let the old heart of him who is forgotten / beat within me'. The perplexing 'waves' of Canto I are revealed and reinterpreted now in Canto XI as being part of the sea of humanity; the inverted tower becomes a well where the 'submerged truths' turn out not to be obscure and personal alone but public and illuminating essentially. The discoveries of this poem are discoveries both metaphysical and political, discoveries which each revolutionary consciousness has to make in its own way but always to one end.

Poetry becomes, as Canto XII makes clear, the business of exploding the self and expanding out to contain and

15

express the whole reconstructed story of the coming to consciousness of an individual and of humankind. It becomes the business of creating a means to 'join together across the earth / all the silent scattered lips'. By making links, by connecting images, ideologies and emotions, Neruda — as all these poems in *Let the Rail Splitter Awake and other poems* hope to show — is staging a complex but direct demonstration with chants that are now heard from South to North, building a monument to a compelling cause which might unite East and West.

Christopher Perriam
University of Durham, April 1988

Let the Rail Splitter Awake
and other poems

LET THE RAIL SPLITTER AWAKE

I

WEST of the Colorado river is a place I love.
I turn towards it, with everything that lives in me,
with all that I was, and am, and believe.
There are tall red rocks, made structures
by the savage air with its thousand hands,
and the scarlet sky arose from the abyss
into them to become copper, fire and strength.
America, stretched like a buffalo hide,
aerial, clear night of gallop,
there, towards the starred summits
I drink your cup of green dew.

Yes, through acrid Arizona and knotty Wisconsin,
to Milwaukee upraised against wind and snow,
in the hot swamps of West Palm,
near the pine groves of Tacoma, in the dense
steel aroma of your woods,
I walked upon mother earth,
blue leaves, stones beneath waterfalls,
hurricanes trembling like music,
rivers in prayer like monasteries,
wild geese and apples, land and water,
infinite stillness wherein the wheat is born.

There, from within my central rock of being
I could extend my eyes, ears, hands on the air
until I heard books, engines, snow, struggles,
factories, graves, plants, footsteps,
and from Manhattan the moon on a ship,
the song of the weaving machine,
the iron spoon that devours earth,
the drill that strikes like a condor

19

and all that oppresses, cuts, sews, runs:
people and wheels in continuous motion and birth.

I love the farmer's small home. New mothers
asleep, fragrant as tamarind syrup: freshly ironed cloth:
fires burning in a thousand homes
surrounded by onion fields.
(The men when they sing down near the river
have voices rough as the stones on its bottom:
tobacco arose from its wide leaves
and like a fiery goblin entered these homes.)
Come into Missouri, look at its cheese and grain,
at the fragrant boards red as violins,
the man navigating a barley-field,
the newly-broken, blue-black colt
that scents bread and alfalfa:
bells, poppies, blacksmiths' forges,
and in the jumble of sylvan cinemas
love bares its teeth
in a dream born of earth.
It is your peace that we love, not your mask.
Your warrior's face is not handsome.
You are vast and beautiful, North America.
Your origin is humble like a washerwoman's,
white, beside your rivers.
Shaped in the unknown,
it is your peace of honeycomb that is most sweet.
We love your man whose hands are red
from the clay of Oregon, your Negro son
who brought you his music born
in the ivory zones, we love
your city, your substance,
your light, your machinery, the energy
of the West, the tranquil honey
of apiary and small town,
the husky boy riding a tractor,
the oat-fields you inherited
from Jefferson, the roaring wheel
that measures out your oceanic territory,
factory smoke and the kiss number a thousand

of a new settlement:
your industrious blood is what we love:
your worker's hand grimed with oil.

Under the prairie night, since long ago,
resting on a buffalo hide in grave silence
are the syllables, the song
of what I was before being, of what we were.
Melville is a marine yew-tree, from his branches
springs a curve of prow, an arm
of wood and ship. Whitman endless
as the fields of grain, Poe in his mathematical
twilight, Dreiser, Wolfe,
fresh wounds in our own absence,
Lockridge, recently dead, bound to the depths,
how many others, bound to the shadows,
while above them burns the same hemispheric dawn
and of them is made what we are.
Powerful infants, blind captains,
amid actions and foliage at times terrifying,
interrupted by joy and pain,
beneath prairies traversed by traffic,
how many dead on plains never before visited:
tormented innocents, prophets newly published,
upon the buffalo skins of the prairies.

From France, from Okinawa, from the atolls
of Leyte (Norman Mailer has recorded it),
from the furious air and waves, almost all
the young soldiers have returned.
Almost all . . . Green and bitter was their story
of mud and sweat: too rarely did they hear
the song of coral reefs, perhaps they never touched
except to die in the islands, the brilliant fragrant
flowers:
            blood and dung
pursued them, filth and rats,
and a weary, desolate, fighting heart.
But now they have come back, you have received them
in your open, far-reaching land

and they have closed up (those who returned)
like a corolla of innumerable, anonymous petals,
to be reborn, and to forget.

II

BUT they found a guest in the house,
or they brought new eyes (or were blind before)
or rasping branches tore their eyelids
or there are new things in the American land.
Those Negroes who fought with you, hard and smiling,
look:
        men have placed a flaming cross
in their part of town,
they have hanged and burned your brother in blood:
they made him a man of combat, today they deny him
voice and decision; at night the hooded
executioners gather, with whip and cross.
        (It was another story
overseas, in battle.)
        An unexpected guest
like an old gnawed octopus, immense and encircling,
has installed himself in your house, my soldier friend.
The press exudes the ancient venom, distilled in Berlin,
magazines (*Time*, *Newsweek*, etc.) are raucous
yellow sheets of defamation. Hearst
who sang a love song to the Nazis, smiles
and sharpens his claws so that you may go out again
towards the reefs or the steppes
to fight for that guest within your house.
They give you no respite: they want to keep on selling
steel and bullets, they prepare more gunpowder
which must be sold quickly, before fresh weapons
advance grasped by new hands.

Everywhere the bosses now settled
in your mansion enlarge their falanges,
they love Franco Spain and offer you a cup of blood:
(one executed, one hundred): the Marshall cocktail.
Choose young blood: farmers

22

in China, prisoners
in Spain,
blood and sweat in the sugar-fields of Cuba,
tears of the women
in the coal and copper mines of Chile;
next, beat it with energy,
like blows with a truncheon,
and don't forget the ice cubes and some drops
from the song 'Let us defend Christian culture.'
Is this a bitter mixture?
You will grow used to it, soldier friend, and drink it.
At whatever place in the world, in moonlight
or in the morning, in the luxury hotel,
ask for this drink that strengthens and refreshes
and pay for it with a good bill bearing the image of
    Washington.

You have also discovered that Charles Chaplin,
last father of tenderness in the world,
is defamed, and that the writers (Howard Fast and others)
the scientists and the artists
of your country
must submit to being judged for 'Un-American' thoughts
before a tribunal of merchants enriched by the war.
To the remotest corner of the world fear has come.
My aunt reads this news and is frightened,
all the eyes on earth watch
these courts of shame and vengeance.
This is the justice of blood-stained Babbitts,
of the slaveholders, the assassins of Lincoln,
it is the new Inquisition which now arises
not for the cross (even that was horrible, inexplicable),
but for the round gold which rings
on the tables of whorehouses and banks
and which has no right to judge.

Morínigo, Trujillo, González Videla,
Somoza, Dutra, joined forces in Bogotá, and applauded.
You, young American, do not know them, they are
the sombre vampires of our *skies*, bitter

is the shadow of their wings:
        prisons,
martyrdom, death, hatred: the southern countries
with their petroleum and nitrate
have conceived monsters.
        In Chile, in the night,
the hangman's order arrives at the humble, damp
house of the miner. The children
awake crying.
        Thousands are in gaol,
are thinking.
        In Paraguay
the deep forest shade hides
the bones of a murdered patriot, a shot
sounds
in the phosphorescence of summer.
        Truth
died there.
        In Santo Domingo why didn't
Mr Vandenberg, Mr Armour, Mr Marshall, Mr Hearst
intervene to defend the West?
Tormented, aroused in the night, why was
the President of Nicaragua driven to flight,
to death in exile?
(Bananas must be defended there, not liberties,
and Somoza will suffice for this.)
        These great
victorious ideas penetrate Greece and China
to aid governments stained like dirty carpets.
        Ah, Soldier!

III

I ALSO go beyond your lands, America,
there I make my wandering home, flying, travelling,
    singing
and conversing throughout the days.
And in Asia, in the USSR, in the Urals I pause
and expand my soul permeated with solitude and resin.
I love whatever man has created in space

by blow of struggle and love.
My house in the Urals is still surrounded
by the ancient night of pines
and silence like a tall beehive.
          Here, wheat and steel
were born from the hand of man, from his breast.
And singing of hammers enlivens the aged woods
like a blue phenomenon.
From here I look across wide regions of man,
a geography of children and women, of factories,
love and songs, of schools
which gleam like violets in the forest
where the wild fox lived until yesterday.
From this point my hand, as if across a map,
traces the green of meadows, the smoke
of a thousand workshops, the smell
of textiles, the marvel
of harnessed energy.
In the afternoons I return
along new, freshly-laid roads
and enter kitchens
where cabbage is boiling, and from where
a new spring will flow for the world.

Here too the young men returned
but many millions were left behind,
swollen, hanging from gallows,
burned in special ovens,
destroyed so that nothing remains
but their names in the memory.
Their villages too were murdered:
the Soviet earth was murdered:
millions of glass bits and bones were mingled,
cattle and factories, even Spring disappeared
swallowed up by the war.
Even so, the young men returned.
And love for the country they had built
was merged in them with so much blood
that they speak *My Land* with their veins,
Soviet Union they sing with their blood.

The voice of the invaders from Berlin
still echoed loudly when they returned
to help the cities, animals and Spring
in their rebirth.

Walt Witman, lift up your grassy beard,
look with me from this wood,
from these fragrant heights,
what do you see, Walt Whitman?
I see, my wise brother tells me,
how factories are working in that city
remembered by the dead,
in pure resplendent Stalingrad.
I see how from the embattled plains,
from the suffering and the flames,
in the humid morning there is born
a tractor which clanks towards the fields.
Give me your voice and the strength of your buried breast,
Walt Whitman, and the solemn roots that are your face
so as to sing of these reconstructions!
Together we will pay homage to what arises
from all the grief, to what surges up
from the deep silence, from the sombre
victory.
      Stalingrad, your steel voice emerges,
floor by floor hope is rebuilt
like a collective house
and again a deep vibration is on march
teaching
singing
building.
Stalingrad emerges from blood
like an orchestra of water, stone and iron,
and bread is reborn in the bakeries,
Spring in the schools, the wind climbs
new scaffoldings, new trees,
while the stern old Volga throbs quietly.
      These books
in fresh shelves of pine and cedar
reunite above the graves

of dead hangmen,
these theatres built among ruins
cover martyrdom and resistance:
books clear as monuments:
one book over every hero
over every millimeter of death
over every petal of this immutable glory.

Soviet Union, if we could gather up
all the blood spilled in your struggles,
all you gave as a mother to the world
so that freedom, dying, might live,
we would have a new ocean
larger than any other
deeper than any other
vibrant as all rivers
active as the fire of Araucanian volcanoes.
Sink your hand into this sea,
man of every nation,
then withdraw and drown in it
all that has forgotten, outraged,
lied and stained,
all that joined the hundred small curs
of the Western dump-heap
and insulted your blood,
Mother of free men!

From the fragrant Ural pines
I watch the library which is being born
in the heart of Russia,
the laboratory in which silence itself works,
I watch trains carrying lumber and songs
to new cities,
and in this balsamic peace a beat starts
as if in a new breast,
girls and doves return to the steppe
disturbing its whiteness,
orange trees become peopled with gold,
now, at each dawn
the market-place has a new aroma,

a new aroma which arrives from the high lands
where martyrdom was greater,
the map of plains trembles
with engineers writing their numbers,
and aqueducts twist like long serpents
across the earth of a new misty winter.

Within three rooms of the ancient Kremlin
lives a man named Joseph Stalin.
The light goes out late in his room.
The world and his country give him no rest.
Other heroes have brought a country into being;
beyond this, he helped to conceive his
and construct it
and defend it.
His immense land, therefore, is part of himself
and he cannot rest because she does not.
In other times snow and gunpowder
found him facing the old bandits
who wished (as again now) to revive
the knout and misery, the anguish of serfs,
the dormant pain of millions of poor.
He was against the Wrangels and Denikins
sent by the West to 'defend culture.'
They were stripped of their hides there, those
defenders of the hangmen, and throughout the wide
lands of the USSR Stalin worked day and night.
But later in a leaden wave came
the Germans fattened up by Chamberlain.
Stalin confronted them at all the vast frontiers,
in all their retreats, in all their advances,
and as far as Berlin, like a hurricane of people
his sons arrived, bringing the broad peace of Russia.

Molotov and Voroshilov are there,
I see them with the others, the high generals,
the indomitable ones.
Firm as snow-covered oak-groves.
None of them has palaces.
None of them has regiments of slaves.

None of them was made wealthy by the war,
by selling blood.
None of them like a peacock
travels to Rio de Janeiro or Bogotá
to command petty satraps, blood-stained torturers.
None of them has two hundred suits,
none of them owns shares in armament factories,
and all of them own shares
in the joy and construction
of that immense country where dawn resounds
arising from the night of death.

They said 'comrade' to the world.
They made the carpenter king.
No camel shall pass through this needle's eye.
They cleansed the villages.
Divided the land.
Elevated the serf.
Eliminated the beggar.
Annihilated the cruel.
Brought light into the deep night.

Because of this, Arkansas boy, or rather
you, gilded youth of West Point, or better
you, Detroit mechanic, or instead
you, stevedore of old New Orleans, to all of you
I speak and say this: walk firmly,
open your ear to the vast human world,
it is not the elegant gentlemen of the State Department
nor the ferocious steel barons who are
speaking to you
but a poet from the extreme south of America
son of a railroad worker from Patagonia,
American as the Andean air,
today a fugitive from a country wherein
prison, torture, and anguish rule,
while copper and oil gradually transform
into gold for the foreign lords.
        You are not the idol
who carries gold in one hand

and in his other the Bomb.
        You are
what I am, what I was, what we must
protect, the fraternal sub-soil
of pure America, the simple
men of streets and roadways.
My brother Juan sells shoes
just like your brother John,
my sister Juana peels potatoes
just like your cousin Jane,
and my blood is of miners and sailors
like your blood, Peter.
You and I will open doors
so that the Ural air will blow
through the curtains of ink,
you and I will tell the infuriated:
'My dear fellow, just this far and no further,'
for beyond, the land belongs to us
and no whistle of machine-gun will be heard there,
but a song, another song, and another.

IV

BUT IF you arm your hosts, North America,
to destroy this pure border
and send the Chicago slaughterer
to govern the music and order
which we love,
        we will emerge from stones and air
to bite you,
        we will emerge from the last window
to fire upon you,
        we will emerge from the deepest waves
to stab you with thorns,
        we will emerge from the furrows so that the seed
can smash like a Colombian fist,
        we will emerge to deny you bread and water,
        we will emerge to burn you in hell.

Don't set foot in gentle France then, soldier,

for we will be there to see that the green vines
shall give vinegar and the poor girls
shall point out to you the spot
where German blood is still fresh.
Don't climb the dry mountain ranges of Spain
for every rock will turn into flame,
and there the valiant fight for a thousand years:
don't get lost among the olive trees
for you will never return to Oklahoma, and don't enter
Greece, because even the blood you are shedding there
today
will rise up and stop you.
Don't come fishing in Tocopilla
Because the sword-fish will know of your plunder
and the obscure miner from Araucania
will seek out the ancient cruel arrows
buried and awaiting new conquistadors.
Don't trust the gaucho singing his *vidalita*
nor the packinghouse workers, they
will be everywhere with eyes and fists,
like the Venezuelans who will wait for you
a bottle of petroleum in one hand, in the other a guitar.
Do not enter Nicaragua either,
Sandino sleeps in the forest until your coming,
his rifle covered with lianas and rain,
his face without eyelids,
but the wounds where you killed him are alive
like the hands of Puerto Rico which wait
for the light of knives.
                    The world will be implacable towards you.
Not only will the islands be deserted but also the air
which now hears words that it loves.

Don't dare demand manflesh
from lofty Peru: in the ragged mist of ruins
our blood's gentle ancestors sharpen their
amethyst swords against you, and in the valleys
sound the hoarse conch-shells of battle, calling
together warriors with their slings, the sons
of Amarú. Nor along the Mexican sierras

need you search for men, to bring them into combat
against the dawn. For the rifles of Zapata are not sleeping,
they are oiled and aimed at the Texas plains.
Do not enter Cuba, where in the ocean glare,
in the sweaty sugar-cane fields,
one single dark glance awaits you
and a single cry, until it dies or kills.
        Do not advance
to the Partisan lands in murmurous Italy:
don't pass beyond the rows of soldiers in slick uniforms
that you maintain in Rome, don't go past Saint Peter's:
beyond that the rustic village saints,
the marine and fishing saints,
love the great country of steppes
where the world flowered anew.
        Do not approach
the bridges of Bulgaria, they won't let you pass;
in the rivers of Rumania, we will throw boiling blood
to scald the invaders;
do not hail the farmer who now knows the tomb
of his feudal lords, who with his plow
and rifle stands guard, do not look at him
for he will burn you like a star.
        Do not disembark
in China: Chiang the mercenary will not be there:
but awaiting you will be a forest of farmers'
sickles and a volcano of gunpowder.

In other wars there were ditches filled with water,
then endless barbed wire with prongs and claws,
but this ditch is wider, these waters deeper,
these wires more invincible than any metal.
They are one and another atom of human metal,
they are one and a million knots of lives and lives,
they are the old griefs of the peoples
of all remote valleys and lands
of all flags and ships
of all caves wherein they were piled up
of all fish-nets with which they strode against tempests
of all the jagged furrows of the earth

of all the hells with their fiery cauldrons
of all looms and foundries
of all locomotives lost or assembled.
This wire encircles the world a thousand times:
it seems divided, uprooted,
then suddenly it joins magnets
until it fills the earth.

But even farther on,
radiant and resolute
steely, smiling
ready for song or combat
there await you
men and women of the tundra and taiga,
warriors of the Volga who vanquished death,
children of Stalingrad, giant of the Ukraine,
all one vast high wall of stone and blood,
iron and song, courage and hope.
If you touch this battlement you will fall
consumed like coal in the factories,
and the smiles from Rochester will turn into shadows
that will scatter over the air of the steppes
to be buried forever in snow.
There will come the fighters who from Great Peter to new
    heroes
have astonished the earth,
and they will make of your medals small cold bullets
to whistle ceaselessly across the entire
tremendous land that today is joyous.
And the vine-covered laboratory
will also release the unchained atom
toward your proud cities.

V

LET none of this happen.
Let the Rail Splitter awake.
Let Abe come with his axe
and his wooden plate
to eat with the farmers.

Let his head like tree-bark,
his eyes like those in wooden-planks
and oak-tree boles,
turn to look on the world
rising above the foliage
higher than the sequoias.
Let him buy something in a drugstore
let him take a bus to Tampa
let him bite into a yellow apple
and enter a moviehouse to converse
with all the simple people.

Let the Rail Splitter awake.

Let Abe come, let his aged yeast raise
the green and gold earth of Illinois,
let him lift up his axe in his own town
against the new slaveholders
against the slave-lash
against the poisoned printing-press
against the bloodied merchandise
they want to sell.
Let them march singing and smiling,
the young white, the young Negro,
against the walls of gold
against the manufacturer of hate
against the merchant of their blood,
let them sing, laugh and conquer.

Let the Rail Splitter awake.

Peace for the twilights to come,
peace for the bridge, peace for the wine,
peace for the stanzas which pursue me
and in my blood uprise entangling
my earlier songs with earth and loves,
peace for the city in the morning
when bread wakes up, peace for the Mississippi,
source of rivers,
peace for my brother's shirt,

peace for books like a seal of air,
peace for the great kolkhoz of Kiev,
peace for the ashes of those dead
and of these other dead, peace for the grimy
iron of Brooklyn, peace for the letter-carrier.
who from house to house goes like the day,
peace for the choreographer who shouts
through a funnel to the honeysuckle vine,
peace for my own right hand
that wants to write only Rosario,
peace for the Bolivian, secretive
as a lump of tin, peace
so that you may marry, peace for all
the saw-mills of Bio-Bio,
peace for the torn heart
of guerrilla Spain,
peace for the little museum in Wyoming
where the most lovely thing
is a pillow embroidered with a heart,
peace for the baker and his loaves,
and peace for the flour, peace
for all the wheat to be born,
for all the love which will seek its tasselled shelter,
peace for all those alive: peace
for all lands and all waters.

Here I say farewell, I return
to my house, in my dreams
I return to Patagonia where
the wind rattles the barns
and the ocean spatters ice.
I am nothing more than a poet: I love all of you,
I wander about the world I love;
in my country they gaol miners
and soldiers give orders to judges.
But I love even the roots
in my small cold country,
if I had to die a thousand times over
it is there I would die,
if I had to be born a thousand times over

it is there I would be born
near the tall wild pines
the tempestuous south wind
the newly-purchased bells.
Let none think of me.
Let us think of the entire earth
and pound the table with love.
I don't want blood again
to saturate bread, beans, music:
I wish they would come with me:
the miner, the little girl,
the lawyer, the seaman,
the doll-maker,
to go into a movie and come out
to drink the reddest wine.
I did not come to solve anything.
I came here to sing
and for you to sing with me.

From somewhere in the Americas, May 1948
(*Translated by Waldeen*)

TO MIGUEL HERNÁNDEZ, MURDERED
IN THE PRISONS OF SPAIN

You came to me straight from the East, Goatherd
you brought me
your furrowed innocence,
the scholasticism of ancient pages, an aroma
of Fray Luis, of orange blossoms, of dung
burning in the mountains, and in your mask
the prickly grain of gleaned oats,
and a honey that measured the earth with your eyes.

You also brought the nightingale in your mouth.
An orange-stained nightingale, a strand
of incorruptible song, of leaf-stripped strength.
Ah, boy, gunpowder intervened in the light,
and you, with the nightingale and rifle, walking
beneath the moon and the sun of battle.

Now you know, my son, all that I could not do,
now you know, that for me, in all of poetry
you were the blue flame. Today
I put my face against the ground to listen to you,
to hear you: blood, music, dying honeycomb.

I have never seen race more radiant than yours,
nor roots so tough, nor soldier's hands,
I have seen nothing so alive as your heart
consuming itself in the purple of my own banner.

Eternal youth, rebellious freeman from ages past,
inundated by seeds of wheat and Spring,
creased and dark like innate metal,
awaiting the moment for your armour to be raised.

I am not alone since you died. I am among those
who search for you. I am with those
who will arrive one day, to avenge you.
You will recognise my footsteps among them,
as they hurl themselves on Spain's breast
to crush Cain, so that the buried faces
may be returned to us.

Let them know, the ones who killed you,
that they will pay with blood.
Let them know, those who tortured you,
that they will face me one day.

Let them know, the accursed, who today include your
    name
in their books, the Dámasos and Gerardos,
the damnable, silent hangman's accomplices,
that your martyrdom will not be effaced, that your death
will fall across the full moon of their cowardice.
And those, wreathed in mouldy laurel, who denied
you space on American earth, to extend
the blood-stained lustre of your fluvial crown,
leave them to me, to contemptuous oblivion:
for they wished to mutilate me by your absence.

Miguel, far from the Osuna prison, far from
cruelty, Mao Tse-tung leads your devastated poetry
in combat towards our victory.
        And Prague, humming,
constructs the sweet bee-hive of which you sang;

verdant Hungary cleans out its granaries and dances
alongside the river awakened from sleep;
and Warsaw's naked siren arises, lifting
her crystalline sword as she rebuilds.

And further on the land grows gigantic;
       the land
visited by your song, and the steel that defended
your country are safe, expanding
upon the firmness
of Stalin and his sons.
       Already the light
is spreading to your resting place.

       Miguel of Spain, star
of a ravaged land, I do not forget you, my son,
I do not forget you!
       But I learned life
from your death: my eyes had commenced to mourn,
when I discovered within me
not tears
but inexorable weapons!
       Wait for them! Wait for me!

(Translated by Waldeen)

THE DEAD IN THE SQUARE

I

I DO NOT come to weep here where they fell.
I come to speak to you who are still living;
I address my words to you, and to myself.

Others have died before. Remember? Yes, you remember
others like these, like you, with the same surnames.

In rainy Lonquimay, in San Gregorio,
in barren Ranquil, scored by the spendthrift wind,
in Iquique choked and half-buried by drifting sand,
along the edge of the sea and the edge of the desert,
following the smoke line and the rain line,
from the high pampas down to the archipelagos,
other men have been murdered,
others with names like Antonio, like your name,
fishermen, blacksmiths, people with jobs like yours:

bone and breed of Chile: faces
scarred by wind-lash, gaunt
as the pampas, wearing
the signature of pain.

II

ALL along the ramparts of our fatherland,
bright at the edge of the blank glass-glitter of snow,
hidden behind the maze of the green-branched river,
under the nitrate, under the fuse of the bursting seed,
I found thick-strewn the drops of my people's blood.
And each drop burned like fire.

III

UP TO that time the blood had been always hidden under
    the roots, always washed off and forgotten;
(it was so far away) the rain from the South had soaked it
    into the earth
(it was so long ago), or the nitre had eaten it up when it fell
    on the pampas.
And the death of the people was as it always had been:
as if it were only stones falling
on stony ground, water spilled into water.
From North to South, wherever the dead
were burned or ground to bits,
they were buried in utter darkness;
or piled up in a dense pyramid;
they were burned in the dead of night and in silence
and their ashes flung to the sea.
No one knows where they are: they have no tomb:
the deep roots of the nation have entangled
their martyred fingers, their exploded hearts.
O laughter of Chile, steadfast soul of the pampas,
voices out of the silence: no man living knows
where your murderers hid you from memory.
But on that day when the nation is resurrected
you will leap from the earth to recover your lost blood.

IV

THIS crime took place right in the open Square.
Not in a forest was the innocent blood spilled,
not in the thirsty concealing sand of the pampas.

No one made any attempt to cover it up.
This crime was done in the very heart of the country.

V

ONCE I was in the nitre beds with the unknown heroes
who dig that powdery fertilizing snow
from the hard crust of our planet;
I was there with those men at the time of the great strike;
I remember the proud hard clasp of their earthy hands.
They said to me, 'Look, brother,
look how we live
here in Humberstone, here in Mapocho,
in Ricaventura, in Paloma,
in Pan de Azúcar, in Piojillo.'
They let me gnaw at the miserable roots
that give them all the nourishment they get;
they showed me the packed earth that is floor for their
    houses,
the heat, the dirt, the bedbugs,
and the endless solitude that is their life.
And I saw the diggers sweating at their work
and how they leave the full print of their hands
pressed in the wooden handles of their picks.

And I heard a voice welling up
from the dense base of the pyramid
as if the womb of hell had cried aloud,
and there lurched forth a creature with no face,
a foetus like a mask all splattered over
with sweat and blood and dirt.
And that nameless thing cried to me, saying, 'Wherever
you go, tell of the torment endured
by those on the bottom, O my brother,
tell of your brother, whose whole life
is lived on the rim of hell.'

VI

PEOPLE, here you decided to lend a hand
to the bowed workers of the pampas; you answered them;
you called them, man, woman, and child,
one year ago, to this Square.

And here your blood gushed forth.
In the very centre of the country it was spilled,
in front of the Palace, right in the middle of the street

for all the world to see.
And no one could mop it up:
your red stains remained there
like stars, fixed and implacable.

It was when one Chilean hand after another
was stretching out its fingers toward the pampas,
and your words came from the heart, speaking unity;
people, it was when you were marching in your own
　　Square,
singing the old songs full of tears and hope and sorrow
that the hand of the hangman drenched the Square with
　　your blood.

VII

THIS is the way the flag of our country was made:
out of the rags of their sorrow the people stitched it;
they embroidered it with the shining thread of love;

they cut from their shirts, or perhaps from a fold of the
　　sky,
that patch of blue to hold the star of their country,
and with eager hands they pinned it there like a jewel.

Drop by drop it is turning to fiery red.

VIII

THIS afternoon I call to them one by one.
One by one, come back to our memory
this afternoon in this Square.

Manuel Antonio López,
faithful comrade;

Lisboa Calderón,
though others betrayed you,
we shall march on in your path.

Alejandro Gutiérrez,
the banner that fell beside you
is rising all over your land;

César Tapia,
your heart is alive in these banners,
I hear it beating, beating in the breeze on the Square;

Filomeno Chavez,
I never shook your hand, but your hand is here:
not even death can stiffen a clean hand.

Ramona Parra, beautiful
as a new star in our sky,
Ramona Parra, delicate heroine,
flower stained with blood, dear young Ramona,
girl with the heart of steel, golden-haired fighter,
by your name, Ramona Parra, we swear to continue the
     fight
until your wasted blood flowers in freedom.

IX

THOSE who came to this Square with loaded rifles,
those who came with orders to kill without mercy,
found here only a crowd of people singing —
a crowd made into a people by duty and love

and a thin girl suddenly fell clutching her banner;
a youth spun round coughing through the wound in his
     side;
in the shock of that silence the people stared at them falling
and slowly the wave of their sorrow lifted and froze into
     cold fury.

Afterward they dipped their banners into the blood
and held them up before the faces of the assassins.

X

IN THE name of these our dead
I demand punishment.

For those who spattered our fatherland with blood
I demand punishment.

For him by whose command this crime was done
I demand punishment.

For the traitor who clambered to power over these bodies
I demand punishment.

For those forgiving ones who excused this crime
I demand punishment.

I do not want to shake hands all around and forget;
I do not want to touch their blood-stained hands;
I want punishment.

I do not want them sent off somewhere as ambassadors
nor covered up here at home until it blows over.

I want to see them judged,
here, in the open air, in this very spot.

I want to see them punished.

XI

I MUST speak to those dead now as if they were here.
Brothers: it will go on,
our fight will go on in the land,
in the factories, in the farms,
in the streets the fight will go on,
in the nitre-pits, in the pampas.
In the craters of copper, glowing with green and red,
in the dank caves where coal-seams gleam through the
    dusk,
the battle-lines will be drawn.
And in our hearts these banners,
the witnesses of your death,
will multiply themselves until they flutter
thick as the thrusting leaves of inexhaustible spring.

XII

FOOTSTEPS shuffling a thousand years in this Square
will not rub off the trace of your blood from these stones;
though the babble of countless voices cross this quietness
that bell will echo, tolling the hour of your death;
though rain may rot these walls to their foundations
it will not quench the blaze of your martyred names
nor the dead hand of a thousand nights of oppression
stifle your living hope for that destined day
that we throughout the world, so many of us,
are yearning toward; the final day of suffering,
the day of justice won through bitter struggle;
and you, O fallen brothers, out of the silence
your voices will rise in the mighty shout of freedom
when the hope of the people flames into paeans of joy.

(*Translated by Robert Brittain*)

SONG FOR BOLIVAR

OUR father who art in earth,
in the water, in the air
of all our wide and silent latitude,
everything bears your name, father, in our domain.
Your name the sugar cane raises to sweetness,
bolivar tin has a Bolivar shine,
bolivar bird over Bolivar Mountain,
the potato, saltpetre, the special shadows,
the currents, the veins of phosphoric stone,
all that is ours comes from your snuffed-out life:
your legacy were rivers, plains, and belfries;
your legacy, father, is our daily bread.

Your little corpse of a gallant captain
has stretched into immensity its mental shape:
suddenly your fingers emerge from out the snow,
the southern fisherman brings suddenly to light
your smile, your voice palpitating in the nets.

What colour the rose we grow beside your soul?
Red shall the rose be that recalls your step.
How shall the hands be that touch your ashes?
Red shall the hands be that are born from your ashes.
And what like the seed of your dead heart?
Red is the seed of your living heart.

Therefore the circle of hands is about you now.
Within my hand is another, and another in it,

and another again, down to the dark continent's end.
And yet another hand you did not know
comes also, Bolivar, to clasp your own.

From Teruel, Madrid, Jarama, from the Ebro,
from the prison, from the air, from the dead of Spain
comes this red hand, a daughter of your own.

Captain, you fighter, wherever a mouth
cries Liberty, wherever an ear listens,
wherever a red soldier smashes a brown helmet,
wherever a free man's laurel blossoms,
wherever a new flag decks itself
with the blood of our illustrious dawn,
Bolivar, captain, your face can be discerned.
Again in the dust and smoke your sword is born.
Again your banner is embroidered with blood.
Scoundrels attack your seed anew;
nailed to another cross is the son of man.

But still your shadow leads us towards hope:
the laurel and light of your red army
gazes with your gaze across the American night.
Your eyes that watch beyond the seas,
beyond the oppressed and wounded peoples,
beyond the black burning cities,
your voice is born anew, your hand is born again,
your army defends the consecrated flags,
and a terrible sound of grief precedes
the dawn that's reddened by the blood of man.

Liberator, a world of peace was born in your arms.
Peace, bread and wheat were things born of your blood:
From our young blood that comes from your blood,
peace will grow, bread and wheat for the world that will be
    ours.

I met Bolivar one fine long morning
in Madrid, in the mouth of the Fifth Regiment.
Father, I said, are you or are you not, or who are you?

And looking towards the Cuartel de la Montaña, he said:
I wake up every hundred years when the people awaken.

(*Translated by A.L.Lloyd*)

THE FUGITIVE

I

THROUGH the tall night, through all of life,
from tears to paper, clothes to clothes,
I wandered in those oppressive days.
Fugitive from the police,
in the hour of clarity, the denseness
of solitary stars, I passed through cities,
woods, small farms, ports,
from the door of one human being
to another, from the hand of one being
to another, and another.
Night is sombre, but man provides
his brotherly signals;
blindly I was led by roads and shadows
up to the lighted door, to the small
star-point that was mine, to
the scrap of bread in the forest
that wolves had not yet devoured.

One night I came to a house
in open fields, and before then
no one had seen or even surmised
about those lives.
All that they did, their hours,
were new knowledge to me.
I entered, they were a family of five:
all had risen as if awakened
by a fire in the heart of the night.
        I took one hand
then another, I saw one face
then another, and they told me
nothing: they were doors I had never glanced
at in the street, eyes that did not
recognise my face, and
in the high, newly arrived night
I stretched out my weariness,
to hold the grievous vigil of my land.

While waiting sleep, earth
with its numerous echoes,
its hoarse clamour and tendrils
of solitude, continued the night,
and I thought: 'Where am I?
Who are they? Why do they take care of me
today? Why do they, who never saw
me until now, open to me their door
and protect my song?'
No one replied,
except the murmurs of a leaf-stripped
night, fabric knitted by crickets;
the whole night seemed to tremble
lightly in its foliage.

Nocturnal earth at my window
you brought me your lips
so that I might sleep gently
as if falling upon thousands of leaves,
from season to season, nest
to nest, from branch to branch
until soon I would lie asleep,
at rest like the dead among your roots.

II

IT WAS autumn in the vineyard.
The innumerable grapevines quivered.
Their veiled white clusters
wore frost on sweet fingers,
and the black grapes filled
their small taut udders from
some secret circular river.
The master of the house, lean-faced
artisan, read to me from this pale
earthy book of twilit days.
His kindliness knew every fruit
every trunk, the way to prune
and leave the tree its bare
goblet form.
He spoke to his horses

as if to enormous children,
the dogs and five cats of his household
followed him about,
some arched and slow,
others running wildly
beneath cold peach-trees.
He knew every branch,
every scar on his trees,
and his ancient voice instructed me
while he stroked the horses.

III

ONCE again I sought darkness.
Crossing the city, the Andean night,
the prodigal night, opened its rose
against my suit.
      It was winter in the South.
Snow had mounted its high
pedestal, the cold burned
with a thousand frozen spikes.
The Mapocho River was black snow.
And I, going between one silent street
and another of the tyrant-stained city,
Ah! I was like the silence itself,
watching love and more love pour
through my eyes into my breast.
Because this and that other street
and the snow-capped lintel of night,
the nocturnal aloneness of human beings,
and my own dark submerged people
in their tenements of the dead,
everything, the last window with its small
twig of false light,
the crushed black coral
of dwelling against dwelling-place,
the unwearying wind of my land,
all was mine, all
in the silence uplifted to me
an abundant mouth of love.

A YOUNG couple opened another door
that was also unknown to me.
           She was as golden
as the month of June, he
a tall engineer. From then on
I shared their bread and wine,
           little by little
I reached their unknown intimacy.
They told me: 'We had
separated,
our misunderstanding was for ever;
today we joined each other to receive you,
today we waited for you together.'
In that small house
we united to make
a silent fortress.
Even in sleep, I kept
silence.
I was in the very palm
of the city and could almost hear
the Traitor's steps; next to the walls
dividing us, I listened
to the gaolers' filthy voices,
their robbers' roars of laughter,
their drunken syllables intermixed
with bullets within my country's body.
The belchings of Holgers and Poblete
almost grazed my soundless skin,
their dragging steps all but touched
my heart and its fires:
they sending my people to torment,
I guarding the sword of my health.
And again in the night, 'Adiós Irene,
adiós Andrés, adiós new friend,'
adiós to the scaffoldings, the star,
adiós perhaps, to the uncompleted house
in front of my window that seemed
inhabited by linear phantoms,

adiós to the soaring mountain peak
which drew my eyes each afternoon,
adiós to the green neon sign
whose lightning announced
each new night.

V

ANOTHER time, another night, I went
further on; along the coastal mountain-range,
the wide margin near the Pacific,
then among twisted streets,
lanes and alleyways: Valparaíso.
I entered a seaman's home.
His mother was waiting for me.
— 'I didn't know until yesterday, she said.
My son told me and your name
rushed through me like cold fire.
But I said, What comforts, son,
can we offer him? — He belongs
to us, to the poor, he replied.
He will not look down upon nor mock
our poor life, he upraises
and defends it. — I told him, — so be it,
and this is his home from today on.'
In that house, none knew me.
I looked at the clean tablecloth,
the water-jar limpid as those lives
which rose from the deepest night
to reach me on crystal wings.
I went to the window: Valparaíso
opened its thousand tremulous eyelids,
the nocturnal sea air
flowed into my mouth,
the lights on the hills,
the shimmer of nautical moon
on the water, the darkness
like a kingdom ablaze
with green diamonds,
all the new repose which life

bestowed on me.
        I looked about: the table
was set: bread, napkin, wine, water,
and a fragrance of earth and tenderness
misted my soldier's eyes.
Beside that window in Valparaíso
I spent my nights and days.
The seamen of my new home
daily hunted a ship
which would take them.
        Time after time
they were deceived.
        The *Atomena*
could not carry them, nor the *Sultana*.
They explained to me: if they gave a bribe
to one or the other official, others
paid more.
        Everything was rotten
as in the Palace at Santiago.
Here the pockets of a corporal
or Secretary open not so wide
as the pockets of the President,
but enough to gnaw
at the skeletons of the poor.
Unhappy republic, dog thrashed
by thieves, howling alone
on the highways, flogged by police.
Unhappy nation, Videla-ridden,
flung by sordid gamblers
to the vomit of informers,
sold on broken street corners,
dismantled at foreign auction.
Tragic republic in hands of a man
who sold his own daughter,
and delivered up his country
wounded, mute, and manacled.
The two sailors came and went,
to haul sacks, bananas, food,
while hungering for the salt of waves,
marine bread, the tall sky.

During my lonely day the sea
withdrew; so I turned
to the hills, vitally aflame
with their overhanging houses,
the pulse of Valparaíso:
high hills overflowing
with lives, doors painted
turquoise, scarlet, pink,
toothless staircases,
clusters of poor doorways,
dilapidated shacks,
the fog, its vapours casting
brackish nets over everything,
trees desperately gripping
the cliffs,
wash hanging from the arms
of inhuman houses,
the sudden hoarse whistle:
offspring of embarkations,
the marine voice compounded
of crashes and whispers,
all this enveloped my body
like a new terrestrial garment,
as I inhabited the high mist,
the lofty town of the poor.

VI

WINDOW in the hills, cold
tin-ore Valparaíso, shattered
into stones and cries of the people!
Watch with me from my hiding-place
the grey harbour ornamented
with vessels, the moonlit water
barely heaving,
the motionless deposits of iron.

At an hour long past
your sea, Valparaíso, was populated
by slender sailing-ships, proud

five-masted clippers rustling
with wheat, dispensing saltpetre,
coming to you from nuptial oceans,
heaping your storerooms.
Tall schooners of nautical high-noon,
merchant craft, banners
swollen by oceanic night,
bearing ebony and smooth clarity
of ivory, aromas of coffee
and nights beneath other moons,
Valparaíso, they approached your
perilous peace, enfolding you
in perfume. The *Potosí*
with its nitrates shuddered
as it advanced over the sea:
fish and arrow, blue turbulence,
delicate whale, towards other
dark harbours of the earth.
All the southern night above
the furled sails, above the
stamen-nipples of the bow,
when, over the Lady of the figurehead,
face of those plunging prows,
the whole Valparaisan night
the world's antarctic night, descended.

VII

IT WAS dawn of saltpetre on the pampas.
The nitrous planet shook
until Chile was loaded like a ship
with crystallized holds.
Today I saw what remained
of all those who had passed
leaving no trail on the Pacific sands.
       Look at what I see,
the derelict debris that slung around
my country's throat, like a necklace
of pus, the rainfall of gold.
Traveller, let my immobile stare

accompany you, inseparable
from the sky of Valparaíso.
The Chilean lives between
garbage and antarctic winds,
dark son of a harsh land.
Cracked window-panes, broken roofs,
demolished walls, sunken door,
leprous whitewash, clay floor
clinging to thin
hillside soil.
Valparaíso, impure rose,
tainted marine coffin!
Wound me not with your thorny
streets, your crown of sour
alleyways, don't let me see
the child maimed by misery
in your deadly swamp!
In you I suffer for my people,
for all my American fatherland,
for all they have scraped from your
bones, leaving you covered with scum,
a wretched ruined goddess
upon whose sweet ravaged breast
ravenous dogs urinate.

VIII

VALPARAÍSO, I love all that you enclose,
all your irradiations, ocean-bride,
even beyond your quiet nimbus.
I love the violent light you shed
for the sailor on a night-sea,
then you are luminous, naked,
flame and mist, lemon-blossoms
in shape of a rose.
Let no one defend you, nor
advance with furious hammer
to strike what I love;
none but myself for your secrets:
none but my voice for your opalescent

strands of dew, for your worn stairways
where the salt maternity of sea
kisses you, none but my lips
against your cold siren's crown
aloft in the air of your summits,
my oceanic beloved, Valparaíso.
Queen of the world's sea-coasts,
central hub of ships and waves,
you are inside me like the moon,
or slant of air through a grove.
I love your criminal alleys,
your blade of moon above the hills,
and your plazas where sailors ashore
reclothe the spring in blue.
I beg you, my harbour, understand
that mine is the privilege to write you
about good and evil,
for I am like a merciless lamp
illuminating broken bottles.

IX

I HAVE travelled celebrated seas,
hymeneal wreaths of many islands,
I am the sea-faring poet,
journey to journey I reached
the farthest foam,
but you, pervasive marine love,
were moored in me as none other.
You are the mountainous capital
of the vast ocean,
along your cerulean flank of centaur
your outskirts glow
with the red and blue paint
of toyshops.
You would fit into a nautical bottle
with your small houses and the cruiser *Latorre*
like a grey flatiron poised on a sheet,
were it not that the wild storms

of the mightiest sea,
        the green gales
of glacial winds, the torment
of your battered lands, the subterranean
horror, the surf of all the sea
surging against your upheld torch,
made of you a magnitude of shadowed
rock, a hurricane-wrought cathedral
of ocean spray.
I declare my love to you, Valparaíso,
and will return to live at your crossroads
when both you and I
are free again. You
upon your throne of wind and wave, I
upon my humid philosophical lands.
We will watch liberty uprise
between ocean and snow.
Valparaíso, lone queen,
alone in the solitude of the solitary
austral ocean,
        I discerned every yellow crag
on your highlands,
I felt your torrential pulse,
your longshoreman hands embraced me
as my soul required
in that hour of night, and I remember
you regnant in the brilliance
of blue fire scattered
by the spray-sparks of your reign.
There is no other like you upon the sands,
southern albacore, queen of the waters.

X

SO NIGHT after night
in that long sombre hour darkening
the whole littoral of Chile,
I went from door to door,
a fugitive.

Other humble houses, other hands
in every furrow of our land
waited for my footsteps.
          A thousand times
you passed that doorway, and it told you
nothing, that unpainted wall, those
windows with wilted flowers.
This secret was for me;
pulsating for me; it was
in the coal mining regions,
impregnated with martyrdom;
it was in the coastal ports
close to the antarctic archipelago;
listen: perhaps it was along
that clamorous street, amid the
noonday music of street-sounds,
or in that window next to the park
indistinguishable from other windows,
but awaiting me
with a bowl of clear soup
and its heart laid on the table.
All doors were mine,
all said: 'He is my brother,
bring him to this poor house'
while my country was like
a bitter wine-press, stained
by so much torture.
The little tinsmith came,
the mother of those young girls,
the ungainly farmer,
the soap-maker, the gentle
woman novelist, the young boy
nailed like a bug to his dreary
office, they all came and their doors
held a secret signal, a key guarded
like a tower, so that I might enter
abruptly, night, day or afternoon
and without knowing anyone could say:
'Brother, you know who I am,
I believe you were expecting me.'

XI

WHAT can you do, Traitor, against the air?
What can you do, Traitor, against all
that flowers and flourishes, is still
and watchful, that waits for me
and condemns you?
Traitor, those bought by your betrayals
must constantly be showered with coins.
Traitor, you may capture, exile and torture,
and hurriedly pay off
before he who sells repents;
but you can barely sleep
surrounded by your bribed rifles,
while I live in my country's lap,
a fugitive of the night!
How sad your small and slippery
victory! While Aragon, Ehrenburg,
Eluard, the poets of Paris,
the valiant writers of Venezuela,
and others, others, many others,
are with me; you, Traitor
are encircled by Escanilla, Cuevas,
Peluchonneaux and Poblete!
Up ladders raised by my people,
down cellars concealed by my people,
upon my country and her dove-wing
I sleep, dream, and smash your borders.

XII

TO EVERYONE, to you
silent night-beings, who grasped
my hand in the shadows; to you
lamps of immortal light, star traceries,
bread of life, my secret brothers,
to all, to you I say:
there is no gratitude,
nothing can fill your cups
of purity or embody the sun

on banners of invincible spring
like your quiet dignity.
I can only believe
that perhaps I may have merited
such simplicity, a blossom
so immaculate, that perhaps
I am one with you, the self-same,
that particle of earth, flour and song,
that natural dough, that knows
from where it comes, and
where it belongs. I am
neither bell so distant
nor crystal so deeply buried
that you cannot decipher me,
I am simply people, hidden door,
dark bread, and when you receive me
you receive yourself, that guest
so many times struck down
and so many times
reborn.
   All things, all people,
those I do not know, all
who have never heard my name, those
who live along our lengthy rivers,
at foot of volcanoes, in sulphuric
shadow of copper, fishermen and farmers,
Indians, blue beside the shores
of lakes that flash like windows,
the cobbler who asks for me at this moment,
as he nails leather with ancient hands;
you, unknowing, who waited for me
I recognise, to you I belong
and sing.

XIII

AMERICAN sand, solemn planted
field, red mountain-range,
sons, brothers threshed by
the old misfortunes,

let us collect all the live grain
before it returns to earth,
and may the new corn yet to be born
have heard your words and repeat
them, and be repeated.
And sing by night and day,
and bite and devour,
and propagate throughout the earth,
and fall swiftly silent,
to sink below stones
discover nocturnal doors
and once more emerge in birth,
to divide and conduct themselves
like bread, like hope,
like the air that circles ships.
The corn will carry you my song
risen from the roots of my people,
to be born, to build, to sing,
and to become seed again
more numerous in combat.

Here are my lost hands,
invisible still, but you
can see them across the night,
across the invisible wind.
Give me your hands, I see them
above the harsh sands
of our American night,
choose yours, and yours,
this hand and that other,
the one raised in fight, and the one
that returns to be sown anew.

I feel no loneliness at night
in the obscurity of earth.
I am people, the innumerable people.
In my voice is the clear strength
that can traverse silence
and germinate in darkness.
Death, suffering, shadows, frost,

suddenly descend on the seed.
And the people seem entombed.
But corn returns to earth.
Its red implacable hands
thrust through the silence.
From death comes our rebirth.

(Translated by Waldeen)

THE HEIGHTS OF MACCHU PICCHU

I

FROM air to air like an empty net
I went between streets and the atmosphere,
through autumn's advent with its arrival
and departure of new-coined leaves,
between spring and the tasselled wheat
as if inside a falling glove,
where the greatest of loves gives us
what is like a long moonrise.

(I live radiant days amid the storm
of bodies: steel converted
into silence of acid:
nights unravelled to their last dust-grain:
embattled strands of the nuptial fatherland.)

Someone who waited for me among violins
uncovered a world like a buried tower
its spiral sunk beneath all
the hoarse sulphur-coloured leaves:
and deeper, in the geological gold,
like a sword swathed in meteors,
I plunged my tender turbulent hand
into the most genital of the earth.
I put my forehead in the waves
below,
Like a drop of water I slid into sulphuric peace,
and like one blind, I returned
to the jasmine of worn human springtime.

II

IF FLOWER delivers to flower its ultimate seed
and rock preserves its scattered blossom
in beaten raiment of diamond and sand,
man crumples the petal of light he gathers
from relentless ocean torrents

and moulds the palpitant metal in his hands.
And soon, upon the sunken table, between
garments and smoke, like a card-shuffled quantity,
remains the soul:
watchful quartz, tears in the sea
like pools of cold: yet
torment and kill it with paper and hatred,
smother it in the carpet of days,
lacerate it amid hostile clothing of wire.

No: along corridors, air, sea, or roads,
who stands guard over his blood, knifeless
(like the crimson poppies)? Fury has shrivelled up
the sad merchandise of the dealer in human beings,
while throughout a thousand years the dew
has left its transparent letter atop the plum tree,
upon the same waiting branch, oh heart,
oh crushed brow among the caverns of autumn!

How many times in the winter streets of a city, or in
an autobus or a ship at dusk, or at night, in that densest
of solitude: a party, beneath sound of shadows and bells,
in that very grotto of human pleasure, I wanted to pause
and search for the inscrutable eternal vein
that I had touched before in stone,
or in the lightning unleashed by a kiss.

(In the grain it is an amber story of small
burgeoning breasts repeating its tender tale
in endless germinal layers, and ever the same
it threads through ivory, and in water is transparent
fatherland, a bell, from distant snows
to blood-darkened waves.)

I could grasp no more than a cluster of faces,
hasty masks, like an empty ring of gold,
like scattered clothes, children of a furious autumn
that would tremble the wretched tree of frightened races.

My hand found no resting-place

fluent as rivulet or firm
as lump of anthracite or crystal,
to return the warmth or cold of my reaching hand.
What was man? In what part of his open talk amid
whistles and warehouses, in which of his metallic
motions lived life, indestructible, imperishable?

III

THE human being like maize was threshed
in the interminable granary of lost deeds,
of miserable events, from the first to seven, to eight,
and not one death but many deaths came to each:
every day a small death, dust, worm, lamp extinguished
in the mud of suburbs, a small thick-winged death
entered every man like a short lance:
and whether assailed by bread or knife,
the drover, son of sea-ports, dark captain of the plough,
or rodent of cluttered streets:
all grew listless awaiting death, their brief daily death:
and the sad crumbling of their days was
a black cup from which trembling they drank.

IV

DEATH the powerful invited me many times:

it was like the invisible salt of waves,
and what emanated from its invisible flavour
seemed halves of peaks and avalanches
or vast constructions of wind and glacier.

I came to the iron edge, the straits
of air, to the shroud of agriculture and rock,
to the stellar void of final steps
and vertiginous spiral highway:
but, wide sea, oh death! you do not come wave on wave,
but gallop in nocturnal clarity
like the total sums of the night.

You never came scrabbling in pockets, inconceivable
your visit without red vestment:
without auroreal carpet of encircling silence:
without lofty or buried heritage of tears.

I could not love the tree in every being
shouldering its diminutive Autumn
(death of a thousand leaves),
all the false dying and resurrection
without earth, without abyss:
I wanted to swim through the broadest lives,
in the freest river mouths,
and when little by little man refused me
and began closing ranks and doors so that
my flowing hands could not touch his wounded
　　inexistence,
then I went from street to street and river to river,
and city to city and bed to bed,
and my briny mask crossed the desert,
and in the last humbled houses, without light, fire,
bread, stone, without silence, alone,
I rolled over and over, dying of my own death.

V

IT WAS not you, grave death, bird of harsh plumage,
whom the poor inheritor of these dwellings
carried within him between hurried meals, beneath empty
　　skin;
it was something else, a poor petal of devastated cord,
an atom of the breast that did not enter combat
or the acrid dew that did not touch the brow.
It was what could not be reborn, a fragment
of that small death without peace or territory:
a bone, a bell that died within him.
I lifted iodine bandages, sank my hands
in the poor sorrows which were killing death,
and found nothing in the wound but a cold draught
blowing through the vague interstices of the soul.

VI

THEN I climbed the ladder of earth
through the fearful maze of lost forests

up to you, *Macchu Picchu.*

Tall city of scaling stones,
residence, finally, of what earth
did not conceal in her sleeping vesture.
In you like two parallel lines
the cradle of lightning and man
was rocked by a thorny wind.

Stome mother, condors' foam.

High reef of the human dawn.

Shovel lost in the primordial sand.

This was the abode, this is the place:
here ascended the full grains of corn
to descend anew like red hailstorms.

Here the vicuña shed its golden wool
to clothe tombs, loves, mothers,
king, prayers, warriors.

Here at night the feet of man
rested by the feet of eagles, in their high
carnivorous lairs, and at dawn
trod tenuous mists beside the feet of thunder,
touching fields and stones
until they knew them come night or death.
I look at robes, and hands,
at traces of water in the resonant hollow,
at the wall smoothed by touch of a face
that looked with my eyes at earthly lamps,
that oiled with my hands the vanished woods:
for everything, clothes, skin, vessels,

words, wine, bread,
is gone, fallen to earth.
And the air with orange-flower fingers
flowed over the sleepers: a thousand years
of air, months, weeks of air,
of blue wind, of iron mountain-range,
that passed like soft hurricanes of footsteps
polishing the solitary dwelling-place of stone.

VII

ANCIENT dead of a single abysm, shadows of a ravine,
this profundity is measure of your magnitude;
when death came, total, consuming,
did you plunge from the fretted rocks,
the scarlet capitals,
the climbing aqueducts
as if into an autumn,
into a single death?
Today the vacant air no longer weeps,
no longer knows your earthen feet,
has forgotten your jars that filtered the sky
when pierced by knives of lightning,
and the mighty tree was eaten
by fog, felled by gust of wind.

The hand upheld suddenly dropped
from summit to end of time.
You no longer exist, spider hands, frail
fibres, tangled cloth, all that you were
has fallen: customs, frayed syllables,
masks of blazing light.

But this permanence of stone and word:
this city like a goblet, raised up in hands
of all the living, dead, silent, sustained
by so much death, a wall: stone petals struck
from so much life: the permanent rose, the dwelling-place,
this Andean atoll of glacial colonies.

When the clay-coloured hand
became clay, and the small eyelids closed,
full of rough walls, peopled with castles,
and when all of man was wrapped in his burrow,
precision remained, unfurled on high:
the towering site of humanity's dawn:
the tallest vessel for containing silence:
one stone life after so many lives.

VIII

AMERICAN love, climb with me.

Kiss with me these secret stones.

The torrential silver of the *Urubamba*
draws the flying pollen to its silver chalice.
The emptiness of vine, of petrous plant,
of hard garland, soars over
the boxed silence of mountains.
Come minute life, between wings of earth,
while, oh savage water, crystal and cold,
pummelled air, scattering combatant emeralds
you descend from the snow.

Love, love, until the abrupt nightfall,
from the resonant Andean ridges,
towards the reddening knees of dawn,
contemplate the blind son of snows.

Oh *Wilkamayu* of sonorous strings,
when you break your lineal thunder
into white spume, like wounded snow,
when your steep windstorm sings
and castigates arousing the sky,
what language do you convey to the ear
newly out-flung from your Andean foam?

Who seized the lightning of cold
and left it enchained on the summits,

its glacial tears divided
its swift spears shaking
its warlike filaments thrashing
carried along its warrior bed,
startled onto its rocky end?

What do your besieged reflections say?
Did your secret rebel lightning rays
travel before thronged with words?
Who shatters frozen syllables,
dark speech, golden banners,
deep mouths, subdued shouts,
within your slight arterial waters?

Who slashes the floral eyelids
come to watch from along the earth?
Who tosses the dead clusters
down your cascading hands
to flail their harvest of night
into your geological coal?

Who flings the enchained branch over precipices?
Who once more entombs the farewells?

Love, love, touch not the boundary line,
nor worship the submerged head:
let time fulfill its stature
in its hall of choked springs,
and between ramparts and swift water
gather air from the sheer mountain-path,
the parallel laminas of wind,
the blind channel of cordilleras,
the pungent salute of dew,
and climb, flower to flower, through the density,
treading on the outflung serpent.

Within the zone of crags, rock and forest,
dust of green stars, luminous jungle,
Mantur explodes like a living lake
or yet another storey of silence.

Come to my very being, to my own daybreak,
up to the crowned solitudes.

The dead kingdom still lives.

And across the sundial the condor's cruel shadow
cruises like a black ship.

IX

ASTRAL eagle, vineyard of mist.
Lost bastion, blind scimitar.
Starred belt, solemn bread.
Torrential ladder, immense eyelid.
Triangular tunic, pollen of stone.
Granite lamp, bread of stone.
Mineral serpent, rose of stone.
Buried ship, freshet of stone.
Moon-horse, light of stone.
Equinoctial square, vapour of stone.
Ultimate geometry, book of stone.
Iceberg hewn by the winds.
Madrepore of submerged time.
Wall smoothed by fingers.
Roof assailed by storming feathers.
Mirrored boughs, bases of storm.
Thrones overturned by twining leaves.
Régime of the pitiless claw.
Windstorm anchored to the slope.
Immobile turquoise waterfall.
Patriarchal bell of the slumberers.
Chain of vanquished snows.
Iron reclining upon statues.
Inaccessible, enclosed tempest.
Puma hands, blood-thirsty rock.
Shadowy tower, snowy discussion.
Night upraised on fingers and roots.
Window for mists, petrified dove.
Nocturnal plant, statue of thunderbolts.
Essential cordillera, marine ceiling.

Architecture of lost eagles.
Sky-cord, mountain bee.
Bloodied plane, structured star.
Mineral bubble, quartz moon.

Andean serpent, amaranth brow.
Cupola of silence, pure fatherland.
Bride of the sea, cathedral tree.
Salt-branch, black-winged cherry tree.
Frosty teeth, cold thunder.
Clawed moon, menacing stone.
Cold locks of hair, action of air.
Silver wave, time's direction.

X

STONE upon stone: man, where was he?
Air upon air: man, where was he?
Time upon time: man, where was he?
Were you also the small broken fragment
of inconclusive man, of hollow eagle,
that along today's streets, with footprints,
with leaves of dead autumn
tramples the soul until the grave?
Poor hand, foot, poor life . . .
Days of unravelled light
falling on you like rain
on fiesta banderillas, did they
drop their dark food petal by petal
into your empty mouth?
           Hunger, coral of man,
hunger, secret plant, woodcutters' root,
hunger, did your jagged reef
rise to these high crumbling towers?

I question you, salt of the roadways,
show me the spoon; architecture, let me
gnaw with a stick at your stone stamens,
climb all the steps of air into nothingness,
scrape at your entrails until I reach man.

Macchu Picchu, did you lay
stone upon stone, and at the base, a rag?
Coal upon coal, and at the bottom, a tear?
Fire upon gold, and trembling within,
the red raindrop of blood?

Return to me the slave that you buried.
Disgorge from the earth the hard bread
of the wretched, show me the garments
of the serf and his window.
Tell me how he slept when he lived.
Tell me if his slumber
was hoarse, half-agape, like a black hole
in the wall made by fatigue.
The wall, the wall! Tell me if every stone floor
weighed upon his sleep, and if he fell beneath
as beneath a moon, in deathlike sleep!

Ancient America, submerged bride,
your fingers too, emerging from the forest
toward the steep void of gods, beneath
nuptial banners of light and stateliness,
mingling with thunder of drums and spears,
your fingers too, those
that transplanted the abstract rose, the linear cold,
the blood-stained bosom of new grain, up to
the web of radiant matter, the fissured rock,
you too, buried America, did you too, in the
innermost bitterness of entrail, like an eagle,
retain hunger?

XI

THROUGH the confused splendour
through the stone night, let me thrust my hand
and like a bird for a thousand years prisoner
let the old heart of him who is forgotten
beat within me!
Let me forget today this joy wider than the sea

because man is wider than the sea and all its islands,
and one must plumb him like a well, to rise
from the depths with a branch of secret water,
of submerged truths.
Broad stone, let me forget your powerful proportions,
your transcendent measure, your honeycombed stones,
and today let me slide my hand over the geometric square,
over its hypotenuse of stinging blood and scourge.
When, like a horseshoe of red scarab-wings, the furious
condor strikes my breast in the rhythm of his flight
and the hurricane of voracious feathers
sweeps the sombre dust of diagonal staircases,
I do not see the swift bird of prey,
nor the blind cycle of his talons,
I see the ancient being, the servant, the sleeper
in fields, I see a body, a thousand bodies,
one man, a thousand women,
blackened by rain and night, under the black wind,
beside the heavy stone statue:
Juan Stonecutter, son of *Wiracocha*,
Juan Coldeater, son of green star,
Juan Nakedfoot, grandson of turquoise,
rise and be born with me, brother.

XII

RISE and be born with me, brother.

Give me your hand from the deep region
of your far-flung sorrow.
You will not return from beneath the rocks.

You will not return from subterranean time.

Your stone-hardened voice will not come back.

Your chiselled eyes will not come back.

Look at me from the depths of earth,
tiller, weaver, silent shepherd:
tamer of companion guanacos:

mason of defiant scaffolding:
water-carrier of Andean tears:
jeweller of crushed fingers:
farmer trembling in the seed:
potter amid your spilled clay:
bring to this cup of new life
your old buried griefs.
Show me your blood and your furrow,
tell me: here I was punished,
because the jewel did not shine or the soil
did not yield on time its stone or its grain:
point out to me the rock on which you fell,
and the wood whereon you were crucified,
rekindle for me the ancient flints,
the old lamps, the whips stuck to open wounds
throughout the centuries,
and the brilliant bloody axes.
I come to speak through your dead mouth.
Join together across the earth
all the silent scattered lips
and speak to me from below, all this long night
as if I were anchored among you,
tell me everything, chain by chain,
link by link, and step by step,
sharpen the knives that you kept,
place them in my breast, my hand,
like a river of yellow beams,
like a river of buried tigers,
and let me weep, hours, days, years,
blind ages, stellar centuries.

Give me silence, water, hope.

Give me struggle, iron, volcanoes.

Cling to me, bodies, like magnets.

Resort to my veins and my mouth.

Speak through my words and my blood.

(Translated by Waldeen)

A FURTHER NOTE

Neruda repeatedly stressed that writing poems meant taking part in a collective enterprise. Nowadays, writing about his poems means much the same. My debt in the pages you have just read is enormous. Although Neruda sometimes reacted to commentaries on his writing with polite astonishment, with irritation at other times, and much of the time with huge amusement, for anyone who might not wholeheartedly share these feelings, there are three names I would especially mention. Robert Pring-Mill has written a succinct literary biography of Neruda in *Pablo Neruda: A Basic Anthology* (Oxford, The Dolphin Book Co., 1975) (though quotations here are in Spanish) and a short, crystal-clear preface to Nathaniel Tarn's version of *Alturas de Macchu Picchu/The Heights of Macchu Picchu* (London, Jonathan Cape, 1966; New York, Farrar Strauss & Giroux, 1967). René de Costa's *The Poetry of Pablo Neruda* (Cambridge, Mass./ London, Harvard University Press, 1980) is the single most useful extensive study in English (and quotations are translated). I have had no time to remark on the translations by 'Waldeen', Robert Brittain and A.L.Lloyd; for anyone interested in the business of translation, John Felstiner's *Translating Neruda: The Way to Macchu Picchu* (Stanford, Cal., Stanford University Press, 1980) might stimulate some constructive critical thinking about what they have chosen to do (or had to do, being, perhaps, pressed for time). Tarn's version of 'The Heights of Macchu Picchu' makes a very interesting comparison to that of 'Waldeen' too.

José Venturelli (b.1924) also illustrated an edition of Neruda's 'Alturas de Macchu Picchu' (in 1948) and a clandestine, Chilean edition of the *Canto general*. He lives and works in Geneva. A major retrospective exhibition of his work took place at the Musée cantonal des beaux-arts, Sion (Switzerland), in 1986.

BRIEF GUIDE to names and places mentioned in the text:

'Let the Rail Splitter Awake'

Dreiser, Wolfe, Lockridge
> North American novelists

Hearst, William Randolph
> North American newspaper magnate and multi-millionaire, chauvinistic backer of US intervention in Caribbean, especially at the time of the Cuban Revolt of 1895

Morínigo, Iginio
> President-dictator of Paraguay, 1940-48

Trujillo, Rafael Leónidas
> President-dictator of Dominican Republic, 1930-61

Videla, Gabriel González
> Elected to Presidency of Chile with the aid of the Communist Party in 1946, his 'Law for the Permanent Defence of Democracy' in 1948 betrayed the CP by banning it from Chile (see also *Introduction*)

Somoza, Anastasio
> Nicaraguan oligarch-dictator, 1936-56

Dutra, Enrico Gaspar
> Succeeded the infamous neo-nazi Getulio Vargas as President of Brazil in 1948, persuaded Congress to outlaw the Communist Party and established important trade links — with strings attached — with the USA

Bogotá
> The city hosted the crucial 9th Inter-American Conference (1948) where Marshall (see below) and others presented the Latin-American coun-

tries with US plans for counter-Soviet consolidation and out of which emerged the Organisation of American States as a regional grouping at the United Nations: the Organisation's headquarters was at Washington

Vandenberg, Senator Arthur H.
>The Vandenberg Resolution of June 1948 endorsed President Truman's view of a need for a Defence of Free Europe (ie against potential Soviet encroachment)

Armour, Philip Danforth
>Multi-millionaire grain-dealer and proprietor of the Chicago meat packing firm Armour and Company

Marshall, George Catlett
>US Chief of Staff, Secretary of State, Secretary of Defence, played a major role in Cold War politics, drawing up the Marshall Plan for economic recovery in the West (as a defence against supposed Soviet expansion)

Wrangel and Denikin
>Civil War generals of the Russian White Army (1918-21)

Molotov, Viacheslav Mikhailovich
>Chief advisor to Stalin at Yalta and Teheran, representative at Potsdam Conference and delegate to the UN

Voroshilov, Klimenti Efremovich
>Soviet Commissar for Defence, 1925-40, succeeded Stalin as President on the latter's death in 1953

Amarú, Tupac
>Leader of resistance against Spanish invaders, he was chained up and then beheaded at the city of Cuzco on the orders of Viceroy Toledo in 1577

'To Miguel Hernández Murdered in the Prisons of Spain'

Hernández, Miguel
> (See *Introduction*)

Fray Luis
> Fray Luis de León, Spanish poet of the 16th century (see *Introduction*)

Dámasos and Gerardos
> The reference is to Dámaso Alonso and Gerardo Diego, two poets who failed to add their voices to those of Republican sympathisers amongst their contemporaries in the years of the Spanish Civil War (1936-1939); they remained in Spain during the years of Franco's dictatorship

'The Dead in the Square'

López et al
> Victims of the riot squad (see *Introduction*)

'Song for Bolivar'

Teruel, Madrid, Jarama, Ebro
> Key sites of Republican resistance in the Spanish Civil War (the last two being the names of rivers)

Cuartel de la Montaña
> The main focus of resistance in Madrid ('cuartel' means barracks)

'The Fugitive'

Holgers and Poblete
> Collaborators of Videla

The Traitor
> Videla

Escanilla, Cuevas, Peluchonneaux
> Collaborators of Videla